CHILDREN'S AUTHORS

ALVIN SCHWARTZ

Jill C. Wheeler

Checkerboard
Library

An Imprint of Abdo Publishing
www.abdopublishing.com

www.abdopublishing.com

Published by Abdo Publishing, a division of ABDO, PO Box 398166, Minneapolis, Minnesota 55439.
Copyright © 2015 by Abdo Consulting Group, Inc. International copyrights reserved in all countries.
No part of this book may be reproduced in any form without written permission from the publisher.
Checkerboard Library™ is a trademark and logo of Abdo Publishing.

Printed in the United States of America, North Mankato, Minnesota.
102014
012015

 THIS BOOK CONTAINS
RECYCLED MATERIALS

Cover Photo: Copyright ©Alvin Schwartz.
        Reprinted by permission of Curtis Brown, Ltd.
            All rights reserved
Interior Photos: iStockphoto pp. 7, 11, 18
                Copyright © Alvin Schwartz.
        Reprinted by permission of Curtis Brown, Ltd.
            All rights reserved pp. 5, 9
There Is a Carrot in My Ear by Alvin Schwartz. Used by permission of HarperCollins Publishers p. 13
Scary Stories to Tell in the Dark by Alvin Schwartz. Used by permission of HarperCollins Publishers
        p. 15
In a Dark, Dark Room and Other Scary Stories by Alvin Schwartz. TEXT COPYRIGHT (C) 1984 BY
        ALVIN SCHWARTZ. ILLUSTRATIONS COPYRIGHT (C) 1984 BY DIRK ZIMMER. Used by
        permission of HarperCollins Publishers p. 16
Scary Stories 3: More Tales to Chill Your Bones by Alvin Schwartz. Used by permission of HarperCollins
        Publishers p. 20

Series Coordinator: Bridget O'Brien
Editors: Rochelle Baltzer, Megan M. Gunderson
Art Direction: Neil Klinepier

Library of Congress Cataloging-in-Publication Data

Wheeler, Jill C., 1964-
 Alvin Schwartz / Jill C. Wheeler.
    pages cm. -- (Children's Authors)
 Includes bibliographical references and index.
 ISBN 978-1-62403-670-5
1. Schwartz, Alvin, 1927-1992--Juvenile literature. 2. Authors, American--20th century--Biography--
Juvenile literature. 3. Horror tales--Authorship--Juvenile literature. 4. Children's stories--Authorship--
Juvenile literature. I. Title.
 PS3569.C56494Z94 2015
 813'.54--dc22
 [B]
                        2014025405

CONTENTS

Alvin Schwartz

If you love reading scary stories, you have probably read books by Alvin Schwartz. Schwartz made a name for himself delighting young readers with stories of ghosts, ghouls, witches, and more. He sold more than 3 million copies of his books over his long career.

Schwartz wrote about everything from tall tales to **superstitions** to **folktales**. He devoted himself to putting on paper the stories people share at summer camps and family reunions. Schwartz was very popular with young readers. But some parents said his books were too scary.

Schwartz also wrote funny stories and riddles. Many kids loved making their parents groan when they read Schwartz's silly riddles. One is "When is a car not a car? When it turns into a parking lot." Schwartz also enjoyed sharing tongue twisters, such as "the sheik's sixth sheep's sick."

Few authors wrote as much about as many things as Schwartz. The *School Library Journal*, the **American Library Association**, and the National Endowment for the Humanities all recognized his work. Many people credit Schwartz with introducing new generations to American **folklore**.

Schwartz was perfectly suited to writing for children because he remained like a child himself. He and his young readers had shared interests, such as jokes and riddles.

A Writer Grows in Brooklyn

Alvin Schwartz was born on April 25, 1927, in Brooklyn, New York. Brooklyn is a part of New York City. Alvin's parents were Harry and Gussie Schwartz. Harry was a taxi driver.

Alvin grew up in a large, extended family that was full of stories. He was surrounded by games, jokes, songs, rhymes, and tall tales. Alvin developed a **passion** for **archaeology** as well as words. His curiosity and love of learning would follow him throughout his career.

Alvin started college in 1944. He studied briefly at New York's City College, now the City University of New York. In 1945, he entered the US Navy at the end of **World War II**.

After the war, he returned to college. In 1949, he earned an undergraduate **degree** in **journalism** at Colby College in Waterville, Maine. He followed that with a master's degree in journalism from Northwestern University in Evanston, Illinois.

Brooklyn, New York

A Job in Journalism

After graduating from college, Schwartz got his first job. From 1951 to 1955, he worked as a newspaper reporter in Binghamton, New York. During that time, he married a teacher named Barbara Carmer. She later helped him illustrate one of his early books.

The Schwartzes would have two sons, John and Peter, and two daughters, Nancy and Elizabeth. While Schwartz enjoyed working in **journalism**, he needed to earn more money for his family. So, he left the world of newspapers to work in **public relations**.

Between 1955 and 1959, Schwartz worked for several different companies. These included Doremus & Company, the Prudential Insurance Company, and the National Foundation in New York. He did not really like any of those jobs.

In 1959, the Schwartzes moved to Princeton, New Jersey. There, Schwartz worked as director of communications for the Opinion Research Corporation, a market research company.

Schwartz would later use his journalism skills to write for children.

Schwartz enjoyed Princeton, especially the libraries. However, he was less thrilled with his job. Something kept pulling him back to writing. So, he decided to work part-time in his corporate career. He would spend the other half of his time writing.

Exploring Social Issues

Schwartz began his writing career with books for adults. He chose topics with which he was familiar. As a father of four, he was very comfortable writing about families.

One of Schwartz's first books was *How to Fly A Kite, Catch a Fish, Grow a Flower, and Other Activities for You and Your Child*. It gave parents ideas on how to spend time with their children. The book was published in 1965.

The 1960s was a time of significant social change in the United States. As a **journalist**, Schwartz had a keen interest in **social issues**. In 1963, he decided to investigate those topics as a **freelance** writer for children.

Schwartz began writing nonfiction children's books for sale to libraries. In 1966, he wrote a photographic essay book titled *The Night Workers.* He also wrote books about the labor movement, stores, museums, and city planning.

The Night Workers *is about people who have jobs that require them to work at night. One of the featured jobs is at a radio station.*

GETTING FOLKSY

Many of Schwartz's books were funded with money provided by the government. However, these programs eventually ended. So, Schwartz had to change his topic if he wanted to keep writing.

Schwartz had always loved games, sayings, songs, and rhymes. It was not until he was an adult that he realized these things were included in **folklore**. He decided his next book would focus on these types of wordplay.

Schwartz began researching and found the American Folklore Society. The society is a group of people who are **passionate** about folklore. Schwartz met and talked with the members. Before long, he had the material he needed for his book.

A Twister of Twists, A Tangler of Tongues was published in 1972. Next was *Witcracks* in 1973, which became a national best seller. It inspired a second volume. In 1974, Schwartz took on popular **superstitions** with *Cross Your Fingers, Spit in Your Hat*.

Sometimes, Schwartz researched why a certain **genre** got its start. He learned that tall tales grew out of frontier days. Pioneers and settlers faced a lot of big challenges at the time. Schwartz believed they made up tall tales to make their problems seem smaller.

There Is a Carrot in My Ear and Other Noodle Tales *features six short stories based on American, Asian, and European folklore. It is part of the I Can Read series written for younger readers.*

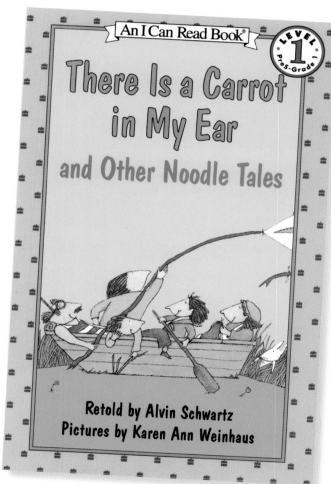

An I Can Read Book®

LEVEL 1 · PreS-Grade 1 ·

There Is a Carrot in My Ear
and Other Noodle Tales

Retold by Alvin Schwartz
Pictures by Karen Ann Weinhaus

How Scary Is Too Scary?

One important part of American **folklore** is the scary story. Schwartz spent a lot of time researching popular scary tales. He often found the same story told in a variety of ways. After figuring out the important parts of a story, he created a new, closely related tale.

Schwartz's first scary book was published in 1981. *Scary Stories to Tell in the Dark* was a hit with young readers. It featured scary drawings from illustrator Stephen Gammell. Schwartz and Gammell would later write and illustrate two more scary books called *More Scary Stories to Tell in the Dark* and *Scary Stories 3: More Tales to Chill Your Bones*.

Some parents thought Gammell's illustrations were too scary. So, Brett Helquist drew new illustrations when the books were re-released in 2011.

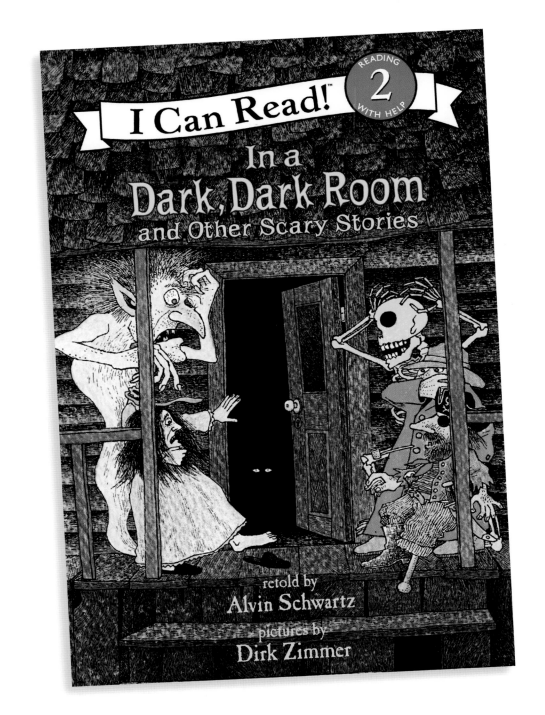

Schwartz believed people started telling scary stories to protect each other. He thought scary stories help people realize the bad things that could happen if they are not careful. He believed scary stories help people talk about their fears.

However, not everyone agrees that scary stories and drawings are suitable for young readers. Schwartz's Scary Stories titles are often included on banned books lists. Some parents feel the books challenge their religious beliefs. Other parents want the books removed from school libraries because they gave their children nightmares.

Yet children consistently claim the books as among their favorites. Many other parents support Schwartz's work. They feel their children's fears will not go away simply because their kids are not reading about them.

In a Dark, Dark Room and Other Scary Stories *is another one of Schwartz's books that has been banned. Some think it is too gloomy for children.*

FRAMING UP FOLKLORE

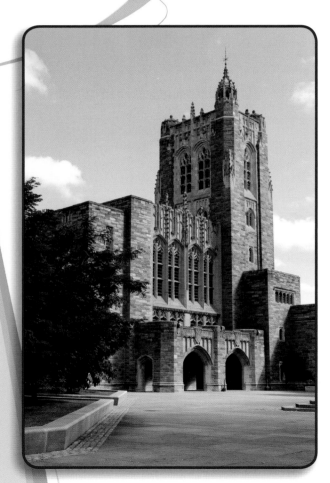

Schwartz rarely worked on one book at a time. He typically worked on three or more **manuscripts**. It helped him avoid getting bored or blocked with any single project.

Schwartz used his training as a **journalist** to help him write. He thoroughly researched all of

Schwartz spent many hours at Princeton University's Firestone Library. There, he was able to research a variety of topics.

his topics and investigated many different sources. Schwartz did a lot of this work at Princeton University's Firestone Library.

While researching, Schwartz looked for patterns. What did many of the **folktales** have in common? What similar elements were present in stories from around the country? He spent about half of his time doing research. The other half he spent writing.

Schwartz's subject matter also required one more important step. Since **folklore** was normally spoken, Schwartz made a point of reading his work out loud before it was finished. He fixed it so it sounded as good aloud as it read on the page. Schwartz even read material to his children to see whether they liked it.

At Home in Princeton

Schwartz wrote his books in a small, converted toolshed near his family's home in Princeton. He was inspired by many subjects, including his community. One book was about local stores. *Stores* was published in 1976.

When not writing his own books, Schwartz taught a writing course at nearby Rutgers University. He worked there for over 15 years. In addition, Schwartz traveled frequently to talk about his **folklore** books.

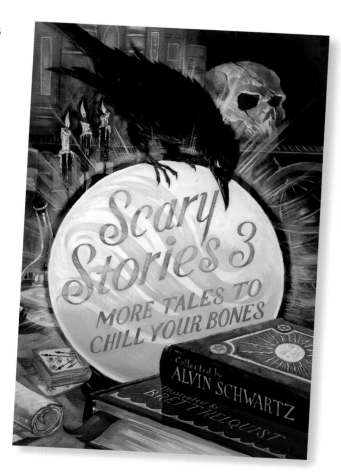

When many people his age were thinking of retirement, Schwartz continued writing. While in his 60s, he wrote two more best-selling children's books. *Ghosts* and *Scary Stories 3: More Tales to Chill Your Bones* were published in 1991.

Schwartz continued to write until his death from **lymphoma** on March 14, 1992. His last book was published that same month. *And the Green Grass Grows All Around* was a collection of folk poetry. It was one of more than 50 books Schwartz had published in the last 30 years of his life.

Schwartz wrote about many topics. He enjoyed speaking to students and educators about them. Today, Schwartz's books continue to share his love of **folklore** with young readers.

Schwartz included his sources at the end of his Scary Stories books. There, he explains his inspiration for each tale and where it came from.

GLOSSARY

American Library Association - an organization whose goal is to promote library and information services.

archaeology (ahr-kee-AH-luh-jee) - the study of the remains of ancient people and their activities. This includes fossils, tombs, and art.

degree - a title given by a college to its students for completing their studies.

folklore - the traditional beliefs, stories, and customs of a community, passed through the generations by word of mouth.

folktale - a story handed down from person to person. A folktale is not usually set in a particular time or place.

freelance - relating to an artist or author without a long-term commitment to a single employer.

genre (ZHAHN-ruh) - a type of art, music, or literature.

journalism - the collecting and editing of news to be presented through various media. These include newspapers, magazines, television, and radio. A person who does this is called a journalist.

lymphoma - cancer of the lymph nodes.

manuscript - a handwritten or typed book or article not yet published.

passionate - capable of or expressing strong feeling.

public relations - the methods or activities an organization or a business uses to promote goodwill or a good image with the public.

social issues - matters that affect some or many people in a community and are considered to be problems.

superstition - a belief that some action not connected to a future event can influence the outcome of the event.

World War II - from 1939 to 1945, fought in Europe, Asia, and Africa. Great Britain, France, the United States, the Soviet Union, and their allies were on one side. Germany, Italy, Japan, and their allies were on the other side.

WEBSITES

To learn more about Children's Authors, visit **booklinks.abdopublishing.com**. These links are routinely monitored and updated to provide the most current information available.

INDEX